T

by Iain Gray

LangSyne
PUBLISHING
WRITING *to* REMEMBER

Lang**Syne**

PUBLISHING

WRITING *to* REMEMBER

79 Main Street, Newtongrange,
Midlothian EH22 4NA
Tel: 0131 344 0414   Fax: 0845 075 6085
E-mail: info@lang-syne.co.uk
www.langsyneshop.co.uk

Design by Dorothy Meikle
Printed by Printwell Ltd
© Lang Syne Publishers Ltd 2019

All rights reserved. No part of this publication may be reproduced, stored or introduced into a retrieval system, or transmitted in any form or by any means (electronic, mechanical, photocopying, recording or otherwise) without the prior written permission of Lang Syne Publishers Ltd.

ISBN 978-1-85217-547-4

Turner

MOTTO:
To be, rather than not seem to be
(and)
For my country.

CREST:
A lion holding in its right paw
a millrind, used to support the
millstone of a corn mill.

NAME variations include:
Turnor
Turnour

Chapter one:

The origins of popular surnames

by George Forbes and Iain Gray

***If you don't know where you came from, you won't know where you're going* is a frequently quoted observation and one that has a particular resonance today when there has been a marked upsurge in interest in genealogy, with increasing numbers of people curious to trace their family roots.**

Main sources for genealogical research include census returns and official records of births, marriages and deaths – and the key to unlocking the detail they contain is obviously a family surname, one that has been 'inherited' and passed from generation to generation.

No matter our station in life, we all have a surname – but it was not until about the middle of the fourteenth century that the practice of being identified by a particular surname became commonly established throughout the British Isles.

Previous to this, it was normal for a person to be identified through the use of only a forename.

But as population gradually increased and there were many more people with the same forename, surnames were adopted to distinguish one person, or community, from another.

Many common English surnames are patronymic in origin, meaning they stem from the forename of one's father – with 'Johnson,' for example, indicating 'son of John.'

It was the Normans, in the wake of their eleventh century conquest of Anglo-Saxon England, a pivotal moment in the nation's history, who first brought surnames into usage – although it was a gradual process.

For the Normans, these were names initially based on the title of their estates, local villages and chateaux in France to distinguish and identify these landholdings.

Such grand descriptions also helped enhance the prestige of these warlords and generally glorify their lofty positions high above the humble serfs slaving away below in the pecking order who had only single names, often with Biblical connotations as in Pierre and Jacques.

The only descriptive distinctions among the peasantry concerned their occupations, like 'Pierre the swineherd' or 'Jacques the ferryman.'

Roots of surnames that came into usage in England not only included Norman-French, but also Old French, Old Norse, Old English, Middle English, German, Latin, Greek, Hebrew and the Gaelic languages of the Celts.

The Normans themselves were originally Vikings, or 'Northmen', who raided, colonised and eventually settled down around the French coastline.

The had sailed up the Seine in their longboats in 900AD under their ferocious leader Rollo and ruled the roost in north eastern France before sailing over to conquer England in 1066 under Duke William of Normandy – better known to posterity as William the Conqueror, or King William I of England.

Granted lands in the newly-conquered England, some of their descendants later acquired territories in Wales, Scotland and Ireland – taking not only their own surnames, but also the practice of adopting a surname, with them.

But it was in England where Norman rule and custom first impacted, particularly in relation to the adoption of surnames.

This is reflected in the famous *Domesday Book*, a massive survey of much of England and Wales, ordered by William I, to determine who owned what, what it was worth and therefore how much they were liable to pay in taxes to the voracious Royal Exchequer.

Completed in 1086 and now held in the National Archives in Kew, London, 'Domesday' was an Old English word meaning 'Day of Judgement.'

This was because, in the words of one contemporary chronicler, "its decisions, like those of the Last Judgement, are unalterable."

It had been a requirement of all those English landholders – from the richest to the poorest – that they identify themselves for the purposes of the survey and for future reference by means of a surname.

This is why the *Domesday Book*, although written in Latin as was the practice for several centuries with both civic and ecclesiastical records, is an invaluable source for the early appearance of a wide range of English surnames.

Several of these names were coined in connection with occupations.

These include Baker and Smith, while Cooks, Chamberlains, Constables and Porters were to be found carrying out duties in large medieval households.

The church's influence can be found in names such as Bishop, Friar and Monk while the popular name of Bennett derives from the late fifth to mid-sixth century Saint Benedict, founder of the Benedictine order of monks.

The early medical profession is represented by Barber, while businessmen produced names that include Merchant and Sellers.

Down at the village watermill, the names that cropped up included Millar/Miller, Walker and Fuller, while other self-explanatory trades included Cooper, Tailor, Mason and Wright.

Even the scenery was utilised as in Moor, Hill, Wood and Forrest – while the hunt and the chase supplied names that include Hunter, Falconer, Fowler and Fox.

Colours are also a source of popular surnames, as in Black, Brown, Gray/Grey, Green and White, and would have denoted the colour of the clothing the person habitually wore or, apart from the obvious exception of 'Green', one's hair colouring or even complexion.

The surname Red developed into Reid, while

Blue was rare and no-one wanted to be associated with yellow.

Rather self-important individuals took surnames that include Goodman and Wiseman, while physical attributes crept into surnames such as Small and Little.

Many families proudly boast the heraldic device known as a Coat of Arms, as featured on our front cover.

The central motif of the Coat of Arms would originally have been what was borne on the shield of a warrior to distinguish himself from others on the battlefield.

Not featured on the Coat of Arms, but highlighted on page three, is the family motto and related crest – with the latter frequently different from the central motif.

Adding further variety to the rich cultural heritage that is represented by surnames is the appearance in recent times in lists of the 100 most common names found in England of ones that include Khan, Patel and Singh – names that have proud roots in the vast sub-continent of India.

Echoes of a far distant past can still be found in our surnames and they can be borne with pride in commemoration of our forebears.

Chapter two:

Fame and infamy

In common with many other surnames found today throughout England, 'Turner' became popularised in the wake of the Norman Conquest of 1066.

An occupational surname, indicating someone who worked with the 'turning' device known as a lathe – used to fashion cylindrical objects, most commonly from wood – it derives from the French 'torner.'

But there are also two other possible sources of origin.

These are from the Old French 'tornei', denoting someone who was in charge of the trials of knightly combat known as 'tournaments', and from a Middle English nickname derived from 'turn hare', indicating someone who was so fleet of foot it was said they could run faster than a hare.

While 'Turner' became popularised after the Conquest, those who had followed the occupation of 'wood turners' had been present in England for a considerable period before this.

This means that flowing through the veins of some bearers of the name today may well be the blood of those Germanic tribes who invaded and settled in the south and east of the island of Britain from about the early fifth century.

Known as the Anglo-Saxons, they were composed of the Jutes, from the area of the Jutland Peninsula in modern Denmark, the Saxons from Lower Saxony, in modern Germany and the Angles from the Angeln area of Germany.

It was the Angles who gave the name 'Engla land', or 'Aengla land' – better known as 'England', while the Anglo-Saxons held sway in what became England from approximately 550 to 1066, with the main kingdoms those of Sussex, Wessex, Northumbria, Mercia, Kent, East Anglia and Essex.

The Turner name is first found in Oxfordshire, while many subsequently went on to stamp a significant mark on the high drama and romance of England's frequently turbulent history.

One particularly infamous bearer of the name was Anne Turner, who was executed in 1615 for her role in the murder by poisoning of the renowned poet and essayist Sir Thomas Overbury.

Born Anne Norton in 1576 in Hinxton,

Cambridgeshire, she had married George Turner, a highly respected London physician.

He died shortly after their marriage and Anne later became a waiting woman and close companion of Frances Howard, the young wife of the Earl of Essex.

In addition to acting as a waiting woman to Frances, the enterprising Anne also had a lucrative business in supplying the saffron-based starch which provided the yellow colouring to ruffs and collars that she was instrumental in making the height of fashion.

Additionally, she is reputed to have also supplemented her income by running at least one 'house of ill-repute' in London while she was also a mistress of the politician Sir Arthur Mainwaring.

Frances Howard, meanwhile, before her marriage to the Earl of Essex for political and dynastic reasons, had become besotted with the young Robert Carr, a courtly favourite of James I, and after her marriage she determined to make him hers.

This required the annulment of her marriage to her elderly husband – so she refused to sleep with him, hoping an annulment would be granted on the grounds of non-consummation.

What stood in her way was the bitter opposition

to any possible match with Carr of the young man's influential friend and mentor Sir Thomas Overbury.

It was now that another character stepped onto the stage of the complex drama. This was Frances's powerful uncle Sir Henry Howard, 1st Earl of Northampton, who used his influence to have Overbury thrown into confinement in the Tower of London on trumped-up charges.

But this was not enough for his niece, because Overbury's influence over Carr still prevailed, and she determined to have him murdered.

Anne Turner now takes her place on the stage of the unfolding drama: using her London underworld contacts, she procured a range of poisons on Frances's behalf that included arsenic and sublimate of mercury.

With a shady cast of other characters involved in the plot, the poisons were mixed into a selection of tarts and jellies and delivered to the Tower to the unsuspecting Overbury. Consuming the sweetmeats, he died, in great agony, in September of 1613.

Frances's marriage was annulled only a few weeks later and she achieved her burning ambition to marry Carr who, reputed to have not been particularly blessed with intelligence or acumen, may have played a wholly unwitting role in the murderous plot.

It was not until two years later, for reasons that remain unclear, that Overbury's murder came to light.

All the main protagonists were brought to trial, including Frances and her husband. They were all sentenced to death but, through their powerful connections, Frances and Carr were later pardoned and allowed to return to their estates.

Not so fortunate were Anne Turner and three others, who were sentenced to hang.

Passing sentence on her the judge described her as "a whore, a bawd, a sorcerer, a witch, a papist, a felon and a murderer."

Adding further insult to injury, he ordered that she be hanged wearing the fashionable starched yellow ruffles she had helped to popularise, "so that the same might end in shame and detestation."

She was hanged in front of a baying crowd at Tyburn in November of 1615, and it is recorded that shortly after this yellow starched ruffles and cuffs went out of fashion.

One decidedly more respectable bearer of the otherwise proud name of Turner was the great English historian Sharon Turner – with 'Sharon', it should be noted, once a fairly common male forename.

Born in Pentonville, London, in 1768 and

originally set for a career as a solicitor, he became fascinated with both Anglo-Saxon and Icelandic literature.

Immersing himself in the study of ancient history, he went on to compile his monumental *History of the Anglo-Saxons*, published in four volumes between 1799 and 1805. Before his death in 1847, he also wrote other noted works that, along with his *History of the Anglo-Saxons*, formed the twelve-volume set *The History of England*.

Bearers of the Turner name have also been ennobled in the Peerage of the United Kingdom.

Born in Yorkshire in 1908, Sir James Turner was the leading figure of the British farming industry who served from 1945 to 1960 as president of the National Farmers Union and also served as president of the Royal Association of Dairy Farmers and the Royal Agricultural Society. Knighted in 1949, he was raised to the Peerage as 1st Baron Netherthorpe ten years later; he died in 1980.

In Australian politics, Sir George Turner, born in Melbourne in 1851, served between 1894 and 1916 as the 18th Premier of Victoria; a founding member of the Australian Natives' Association, he died in 1916.

Chapter three:

Battle honours

Bearers of the Turner name have also gained distinction on the bloody field of battle – no less so than the brothers Alexander and Victor Turner, who were both recipients of the Victoria Cross (VC), the highest award for valour in the face of enemy action for British and Commonwealth forces.

Born in 1893 in Reading, Berkshire, Alexander Turner was a posthumous First World War recipient of the honour.

He had been a second lieutenant in the 3rd Battalion, The Royal Berkshire Regiment (Princess Charlotte of Wales's) when in September of 1915 near Vermelles, France, he led a daring bombing attack on a German communication trench.

His action helped to provide vital cover for his regiment's flank, but he was killed in the attack.

His VC is now on display at The Royal Gloucestershire, Berkshire and Wiltshire Regiment (Salisbury), in Salisbury, Wiltshire.

His younger brother Victor, born in 1900, was a Second World War recipient of the honour.

He had been a lieutenant colonel in the Rifle Brigade (Prince Consort's Own) when, in October of 1942 at El Aqqaqir, Western Desert, Egypt, he was instrumental in the destruction of a number of enemy tanks despite having received a severe head wound.

He died in 1972, while his VC is now on display at the Royal Green Jackets Museum, Winchester.

Born in 1899 in Longview, Texas, George Turner was a Second World War recipient of the Medal of Honor, America's highest award for military valour.

He had been a private with the 499th Armored Field Artillery when, in January of 1945 at Phillippsbourg, France, he performed the actions for which he was awarded the honour.

Standing in the middle of a road and under very heavy enemy fire, he coolly manned and aimed a rocket launcher and destroyed one enemy tank and disabled another.

He then dismounted a machine-gun from a half track and fired into a mass of enemy infantry. Despite being badly wounded, he then drove a truck carrying a number of wounded comrades to a rear aid station.

He died in 1951, while President Harry S.

Truman, when presenting him with his Medal of Honor, told him: "I would rather have that medal than be President of the United States."

Lieutenant General Sir Richard Turner was a Canadian recipient of the VC, along with Lieutenant Zane Cockburn and Sergeant William Holland, for his actions during the 1899 to 1902 Second Boer War in South Africa.

It was in May of 1900 at Leliefontain, while serving with The Royal Canadian Dragoons, that he and the two others managed to drive off a party of Boers who had attempted to seize artillery weapons.

Commander for a time of the 3rd Brigade in the 1st Division of the Canadian Expeditionary Force during the First World War and also the recipient of the Distinguished Service Order (DSO), he died in 1961, aged 90.

Born near Liverpool in 1856, William Turner was the captain of the ill-fated White Star Line passenger vessel the *Lusitania*.

It was on May 7, 1915 that the ship, en route from New York to Liverpool, was torpedoed and sunk by a German submarine about eleven miles off the south coast of Ireland, with the loss of nearly 2,000 lives.

Captain Turner, who survived the sinking, died in 1933, while one of his sons, Percy Turner, was killed during the Second World War when the Royal Navy vessel on which he was serving was torpedoed by a submarine.

From the destructive art of war to the constructive art of medical research, Dr George Grey Turner was the pioneering English surgeon whose early research into cancer anticipated the development of chemotherapy.

Born in 1877 and receiving his medical degree from Newcastle Medical School, he was the author of the landmark 1925 *Some Encouragements in Cancer Surgery*, in which he said: "We shall never overcome cancer by surgery – it will be something we inject."

President of the International Society of Surgeons before his death in 1951, he is also famed for having during the First World War performed one of the earliest operations to remove a bullet from a soldier's heart.

He failed to remove the bullet, but nevertheless still saved the patient's life.

Utilising some of the early research carried out by Dr George Grey Turner, Professor Robert

Lowry Turner, born in 1923, pioneered the chemotherapy treatment that his namesake had predicted.

This was along with fellow surgeon George Whyte-Watson, through work they carried out in the late 1950s from a laboratory in Bradford Royal Infirmary; he died in 1990, while both he and Whyte-Watson are commemorated through a plaque in Bradford Cathedral.

Yet another notable bearer of the Turner name in the field of medicine is Robert Turner, born in 1946 in Northamptonshire.

Among a group of physicists responsible for the development and use of Magnetic Resonance Imagery (MRI) and an expert in brain physics, it was Turner who devised the coils used inside MRI scanners.

The son of the English cultural anthropologists Edith and Victor Turner and brother of the poet Frederick Turner, posts he has held include director of the Max Planck Institute for Human Cognitive and Brain Sciences in Leipzig, Germany.

Still in the world of medicine, Henry H. Turner, born in 1892 and who died in 1970, was the American endocrinologist who identified what is now known as Turner Syndrome – relating to abnormalities in female sex chromosomes.

From the world of medicine to the competitive and challenging world of business, Robert Edward Turner III, born in 1938 in Cincinnati, Ohio, is the American media entrepreneur better known as Ted Turner.

The son of Edward Turner II – who made his fortune from pioneering billboard advertising – and ranked until 2011 as the largest private landowner in the United States, he is best known as the founder in 1980 of the international news media organisation Cable News Network (CNN).

Launching the network from headquarters in Atlanta, Georgia, he famously said: "We won't be signing off until the world ends. We'll be on, and we will cover the end of the world, live, and that will be our last event …"

The first media figure to be named, in 1991, as *Time* magazine's Man of the Year and a recipient of the Albert Schweitzer Gold Medal for Humanitarianism in recognition of his wide philanthropic work, he was formerly married to the actress Jane Fonda.

Chapter four:

On the world stage

Born in 1921 in Wallace, Idaho, Julia Jean Turner was the Hollywood actress better known as Lana Turner.

Signed to a film contract by MGM at the age of only sixteen, her first role was in the 1937 *They Won't Forget*, while further screen credits, as a leading actress, include the 1941 *Johnny Eagle*, the 1941 *Ziegfeld Girl* and, from 1946, *The Postman Always Rings Twice*.

Dubbed by the media at the time as "the sweater girl" because of the tight-fitting and figure-hugging tops she wore, she was also known as one of Hollywood's first "scream queens" – this was thanks to her role in the 1941 horror film *Dr Jekyll and Mr Hyde*.

Other major screen credits include the 1957 *Peyton Place*, for which she was nominated for an Academy Award for Best Actress, while in the 1980s she was a recurrent guest on the television drama *Falcon Crest*.

Married eight times to seven different

husbands – including twice to the restaurateur Stephen Crane, father of her daughter Cheryl Crane – she once famously remarked: "My goal was to have one husband and seven children, but it turned out to be the other way around."

She was at the centre of unwelcome media attention in 1958 when her daughter stabbed Turner's then lover, Johnny Stompanto, to death. A coroner's inquest, however, concluded she had acted in self-defence.

The recipient of a star on the Hollywood Walk of Fame, she died in 1995.

On the stage of contemporary acting **Kathleen Turner** is the American actress born in 1954 in Springfield, Missouri.

The daughter of a U.S. Foreign Services officer, her major big screen credits include the 1981 *Body Heat*, the 1983 *Romancing the Stone*, the 1984 *Prizzi's Honour* and, from 1986, *Peggy Sue Got Married* – for which she was nominated for an Academy Award for Best Actress.

Also a noted actress of theatre, she has been nominated twice for a Tony Award – for her role of Maggie in *Cat on a Hot Tin Roof* and for Martha in *Who's Afraid of Virginia Woolf?*

Her television credits include *Friends*, *Californication* and *Nip/Tuck*.

Born in 1983 in Clondalkin, Dublin, **Aidan Turner** is the Irish actor who first rose to fame through television roles that include Dante Gabriel Rossetti in *Desperate Romantics* and also the supernatural drama series *Being Human* and the series *The Clinic*.

On the big screen, he portrays Kili in the 2012 *The Hobbit: An Unexpected Journey*, while at the time of writing he is also set to appear in the other two planned films in the *Hobbit* trilogy, *The Desolation of Smaug* and *There and Back Again*.

Best known for her role of Stacey Slater in the popular British television soap *EastEnders*, **Lacey Turner** is the award-winning actress born in 1988 in Hendon, London.

Her many awards for *EastEnders* include the 2006 and 2010 Best Actress Award from the British Soap Awards and the 2010 and 2011 National Television Award for Serial Drama Performance.

With big screen credits that include the 1964 *The Black Torment* and the 1976 *The Slipper and the Rose*, **John Turner** is the English actor best known for his role from 1991 to 1993 of Roderick Spode in television's *Jeeves and Wooster*.

Born in London in 1932, his other television credits include *Z-Cars*, *The Saint*, *Heartbeat* and *The Bill*.

Born in London in 1980, **Ben Turner** is the actor best known for his role of the nurse Jay Faldren in the British television medical drama series *Casualty*.

Born in 1960 in Stoke-on-Trent, Staffordshire, **Anthea Turner** is the English television presenter and media personality whose many television roles have included presenting the children's show *Blue Peter* from 1992 to 1994 and as a co-presenter of *GMTV*.

Behind the camera lens, **Alex Turner** is the American film director, producer and screenwriter best known for his cult 2004 horror film *Dead Birds*.

Born in New York City in 1971, his other film credits include the short film *Chuck* – winner of the Rod Serling Award at the 2001 Long Island Film Festival and the 2009 *Red Sands*.

From the stage to music, **Tina Turner** is the American singer hailed as "The Queen of Rock and Roll."

Born Anna May Bullock in Nutbush, Haywood County, Texas, in 1939, the daughter of a farming overseer, her career started in the late 1950s as a singer in the band Ike Turner's Kings of Rhythm.

Marrying Turner, who was born in 1931 and died in 2007, she went on with him to enjoy a string of hits that include the 1966 *River Deep – Mountain High* and the 1977 *Proud Mary*.

Her autobiography *I Tina*, detailing abuse she suffered at the hands of her husband, whom she divorced in 1978, was later adapted for the biographical film *What's Love Got to Do with It* – also the title of one of her solo singles.

Other top hits include *Private Dancer* and *Nutbush City Limits*, while as an actress she has starred in films that include Mel Gibson's 1985 *Mad Max Beyond the Thunderdome*.

The recipient of eight Grammy Awards and having sold at the time of writing more concert tickets than any other solo performer in history, she has been named by *Rolling Stone* magazine as "One of the greatest singers of all time."

Better known as **Big Joe Turner**, or "The Boss of the Blues", Joe Turner was the American blues musician recognised as one of the pioneers of rock and roll.

Born in 1911, his many recordings include the 1938 *Roll 'Em Pete*, the 1951 *Chains of Love*, his famous 1954 *Shake, Rattle and Roll* and, from 1957, *Midnight Special*.

An inductee of the Blues Hall of Fame and the Rock and Roll Hall of Fame, he died in 1985.

In contemporary rock music **Joe Lynn Turner**, born Joseph Linquito in 1951, is the American singer who has performed with bands that include Rainbow, Deep Purple, Brazen Abbot and, along with Glenn Hughes, the Hughes Turner Project.

Best known as the lead singer, vocalist and songwriter with the British band the Arctic Monkeys, **Alex Turner** was born in 1980 in High Green, Sheffield.

Top-selling albums the band has recorded include their 2006 *Whatever People Say I Am, That's What I'm Not* – the fastest selling debut album in British music history – the 2007 *Favourite Worst Nightmare* and, from 2011, *Suck It and See*.

Born in Winnipeg, Manitoba, in 1943, **Fred Turner** is the Canadian rock bassist, vocalist and songwriter who was a founding member in the 1970s, along with Randy Bachmann, of Bachmann-Turner Overdrive.

More commonly known as B.T.O., the band's hit singles include the 1974 *You Ain't Seen Nothing Yet*.

Bearers of the Turner name have also excelled in the highly competitive world of sport.

Born in Greenville, South Carolina in 1956, **Sherri Turner** is the American professional golfer who, after becoming a member of the Ladies Professional Golf Association (LPGA) Tour in 1984, went on to win the 1988 Mazda LPGA Championship and was also a runner-up in the 1999 U.S. Women's Open.

From the golf course to the skating rink, **Roger Turner**, born in 1901 in Milton, Massachusetts, was the American figure skater who won the U.S. National Championship seven times between 1928 and 1934; an inductee of the U.S. Figure Skating Hall of Fame, he died in 1993.

Taking to the water, **Pat Turner**, born in Toronto in 1961, is the rower who was a member of the Canadian men's eight team that won the gold medal at the 1984 Olympics in Los Angeles.

From sport to the creative world of the written word, Ernest Sackville Turner was the British journalist and author better known as **E.S. Turner**.

Best known for his contributions to the British humour magazine *Punch* over a period of more than 50 years, he was born in 1909 in Liverpool.

He was aged 17 when his father gifted him a second-hand typewriter, and this inspired him to pursue a career as a writer – having an article accepted for publication by the Scottish *Dundee Courier* when he was aged 18.

Employed on the strength of this as a copy boy on the *Glasgow Evening Times*, followed by sub-editor, reporter and then gossip column editor, he moved to the *Glasgow Evening Citizen*, followed by the *Daily Express*, until his journalistic career was interrupted by the outbreak of the Second World War.

Serving for a time in the Royal Artillery, the Army put his writing talents to use by assigning him to set up and edit *Soldier*, the magazine of the British Army.

Pursuing a career after the war as a freelance writer and contributing to *Punch* and other publications that include *The Times Literary Supplement* and the *London Review of Books*, before his death in 2006 he also authored books that include his 1952 *The Shocking History of Advertising* and the 1962 *What the Butler Saw*.

From the written word to culinary delights, **Brian Turner** is the British celebrity chef and restaurateur who has appeared on a number of television programmes that include *Ready Steady Cook*.

Born in 1946 in Halifax, Yorkshire, he is the recipient of a CBE for his services to tourism and training in the catering industry and a Craft Guild of Chefs' Special Award for Achievement.

Bearers of the proud name of Turner have also excelled in the highly creative world of art – no less so than Joseph Mallord William Turner, better known as the great British Romantic landscape painter, water-colourist and printmaker better known as **J.M.W. Turner**.

Known as "the painter of light", he was born in London in 1775, the son of a barber and wig-maker.

Taking up the paintbrush at the age of 10, his first watercolour, *A View of the Archbishop's Palace, Lambeth*, was accepted for the Royal Society's summer exhibition of 1790, when he was aged only 15.

Later travelling throughout Europe and studying at the Louvre in Paris, he returned to his native land to produce a stunning series of paintings in his lifetime that include 2,000 watercolours and more than 550 oil paintings.

These include his 1801 *Dutch Boats at Sea*, the 1822 *The Battle of Trafalgar* and his 1839 *The Fighting Temeraire*.

One indication of the regard with which his work is held to this day is that in 2011 the John Paul Getty Museum paid at auction $44.9 million for his 1839 work *Modern Rome – Campo Vaccino*.

He died in 1851, with his last words reputed to have been "The Sun is God."

Many of his paintings are now held in the collection of the Tate Gallery, London, while the prestigious annual art award, the Turner Prize, was created in his honour in 1984.